Mesopotamia

By the same author

Poetry

Downpatrick Races (2000)

The Down Recorder (2004)

Market Street (2010)

Lamentations (2010)

Apparitions: A Hurricane (Pamphlet, 2013)

Drama

Soldiers of the Queen (Lagan Press, 2003)

As Editor

All Souls' Night & Other Plays by Joseph Tomelty (1993)

Martin Lynch: Three Plays (1995)

John Hewitt: Two Plays (1999)

Joseph Tomelty: Collected Plays (2011)

For
Brendan,
old comrades.
D.

Mesopotamia

Damian Smyth

Damian Smyth

30-V-14

Templar Poetry

Published in 2014 by Templar Poetry

Fenelon House
Kingsbridge Terrace
58 Dale Road, Matlock, Derbyshire
DE4 3NB

www.templarpoetry.co.uk

ISBN 978-1-906285-70-8

For permission to reprint or broadcast these poems write to
Templar Poetry

A CIP catalogue record of this book is available from the British Library

Typeset by Pliny

Cover Design and Artwork by Nicola Rowlands

Printed in Europe

Acknowledgements

Thanks are due to the editors of the following journals in which some of these poems, or versions of them, appeared: *Poetry Ireland, The Stinging Fly, Poetry Salzburg Review, The SHOp, Fortnight.*

"And Zelica was left - within the ring
Of those wide walls the only living thing;
The only wretched one, still cursed with breath
In all that frightful wilderness of death,
More like some bloodless ghost - such as, they tell,
In the lone Cities of the Silent dwell,
And there, unseen of all but Alla, sit
Each by its own pale carcass, watching it."

from *Lalla Rookh* (1817), Thomas Moore

"Upon the river's other side there grow
Deep olive groves; there other ghosts abide,
Blest indeed they, but not supremely blest.
We cannot see beyond, we cannot see
Aught but our opposite and here are fates
How opposite to ours"

from *Gebir* (1798), Walter Savage Landor

Contents

PREHISTORIES

HISTORIES

SURVIVALS

PREHISTORIES

Flight into Egypt

after Turner

It really is about being prepared,
after all, to drop everything and run;
or bundle up the belongings gathered
over years on your back like a dolmen

and move off at night taking the back roads
out of the empty ridiculous blue
into the earth's terracotta methods
for vexing miracles of soft tissue.

The precious cartilage of an infant
carried as a sacrifice to the eye:
half fugitive, changeling, half revenant,
the old townlands injured by a sortie.

There is the tale of being put to flight:
hunched figures only God's eyes register
turn from the murders we have to commit
into the half-light, out into Ulster.

Prehistory

What Hugh Killen planned is anyone's guess:
Mesopotamia's Fertile Crescent
chalked up on the board at the start of class
and not referred to, no clue what it meant.

But it was some peculiar Gestalt
where the origins of History threw
a shadow like a psychic somersault
across the single task of getting through

Geography, Spanish, Cartesian graphs;
where that dead land on its salty floodplain
could demonstrate again its secret proofs
under cover like a terrorist campaign.

Or something. Or that handgun in the gutter
Joe Mackin found. Or those lovely gels
on English Street: willowy, unspotty,
those strangers, those Protestants, those gazelles.

Abroad

Foreign lands: the other side of the lough;
poems on the walls of the Arkle Bar;
your Lurgan talk with its 'ack' for 'agh';
nifty southpaw footwork on the dance floor;

the brittle fingers of oleander;
any occasion of unbridled joy;
the prose works of Walter Savage Landor;
your bedside table; something corduroy

among my shirts as if a seal's in there;
your back my fingers criss-cross on patrol
watching TV, my arm under your sweater;
Hugh Grant movies; all things oil and petrol;

and then there is my singing while asleep
of which there is and needs no other proof
than your voice calling me home through the deep
where I'm lost, bewildered and not far off.

Dead Souls

They came the long way to be anywhere
and call it home: the dust of an outhouse
in summer, the bronchi of dead leather
harnesses in exhausted asbestos.

What birds there were had come from Africa
to mutter and build their shit like brocade,
riding the silk road of the Sirocco;
and because they carried souls of the dead,

like the big body of the hare, like seals,
kinds of possession: ghosts rooting the roads
for small lives to explain their travels.
But having come that way, through episodes

we have heard tell of down the centuries,
it's odd how they are inarticulate —
birds, the live things — about all those stories
desperately heard and inaccurate.

Cargoes

Voyages of discovery returned
rich substance from abroad, strange cargoes
of fruit and flora, skin tart and sunburned,
lethargic species from Galapagos

and Easter, survivals of the unique
become commonplace but no less wondrous,
because indifferent no less heroic,
exposed to history with *ad hoc* purpose;

made incarnate in some human scripture.
This is how the consignment of your breasts
just now arrived with us, a rare capture
of the mad and the mundane of other coasts,

still ripe from the journey and gathered in
a menagerie of ankles, shoulders, knees,
long-lived as the turtle, sleek as the dolphin,
fed like a heart on tongue and wild honeys.

Native

Every time I come back I say anywhere
will suffice, any site or locale,
because it is random ceremony,
this wintry agony of the nightingale,

without house or home in the whole island
and one solitary instance of song
in one hundred years, one air disciplined
once by melody in a certain tongue.

Which makes then of my mother's tea towel
a sighting surely, a song sheet of sorts,
a souvenir of wetlands and wild fowl
she had never visited, foreign resorts,

the only place in Ireland where that bird
was spotted with the washing and the whins,
in the crook of her arm, seen and not heard,
with a flick of linen opening its wings.

Monsters

It is ordinary, though, how they lived,
the monsters; uncomplicating our age
as if they judged they should be well-behaved
and we count their days with us a privilege.

Such transformations; such neat escapes from
the rough asylums of the fairytales,
waste-ground, under-stairs, coal-bunker, spare-room,
each place fear set them in as sentinels.

Instead, they crossed with a perfect footstep
our lethal threshold: humans, prodigies,
the white eye turned to a child at the bus stop
a wonder of ailments, with its own liturgies

of origin leaving reverence intact.
O clubbed-foot, hare-lipped, townland idiots,
shopfloor warriors, routine and hunchbacked,
you old gods of our earth in new estates.

Ballygullion

The talk is they grow dope at Bishopscourt
and sell it on Scotch Street. On afternoons,
that's where the city fathers congregate -
old-fashioned winos - turning into bronze,

like those bronze sculptures no one understands,
built because the city needed statues.
Drunks do fashion themselves into legends,
because they persist and are anonymous

and seem not to age but are artefacts,
compass points, familiars, bearings, milestones
and long narratives without subjects
but with not inconsiderable style.

Hence they are remembered down the decades
though no less fictions, no less harum-scarum,
than almond-eyed youngsters at their strange trades
under those tin skies at the aerodrome.

St Dympna's Well

It is harder to believe in the wells,
now all are dead who had trusted in them
and the life-to-come and cures and angels,
except as metaphor and then as stratagem.

It is a lonely mission now: at dawn,
the fields are empty, but the housing scheme
which shelters it comes in to its own
with car doors banging. In the old regime

of wonders, now was time for pilgrimage,
making a way to a hole in the ground
on bare feet, horseback; the antique language
of faith and candlelight for so long trained

to articulate the quiet nothingness
of cold water. If it rolls out its tongue
now, it will be dirty, unscrupulous:
a grace still as useless and unnerving.

Cure

One was supposed to get fleas off hedgehogs,
ringworm from posts. Foxglove gave ganglions,
boor tree rashes. Strangery came from clegs
and incontinence from dandelions.

So much is hidden and all of it true.
You must know now this is how I get by
day after day, on scraps and residue,
in the world I would rather occupy,

where my father's notebook's an almanac
of miracle-workers, sorcerers, Magi.
There lives a man in Crossgar with the knack
of curing your disease. The strategy –

because it's the problem that's the problem
for once and not the cure – is to overhaul
this complex world so shingles takes the blame.
That done, a dead man can expect my call.

Grave Goods

As a child, I thought the dead could hear me
clattering about on their lids above
where they were lying intact as an army
in cells or versions of cave or alcove,

just underfoot. They were holding their breath,
I thought, till I passed by; a hide-and-seek
that was all seek. I thought the aftermath
of death was absence purely, a long break

from the everyday, spent inches under
in the cool larder of earth, its cupboard,
its hospital or its room for repair
from which, in time, the lost would rise restored,

so themselves again you could pick them out.
Not now, of course; the older myths prevail.
At Ardglass, death was decked out like a boat.
Indeed, each grave below raised its stone sail.

Veterans

Mark them out: who made a sort of return,
who shake from head to toe or whoop like birds
or speak in tongues, hide booze in the cistern,
piss in the minibus, sneeze down their beards.

Heroes, as it were; kinds of survivor,
those with white wounds under clothing and skin;
gunshots at night in the corridor,
patrolling the grounds in units of one.

Explain them. Decades after the conflict,
Arab and Boer on the long acres,
tribal catchphrases vexing the district,
children's talk picked-up from quiet speakers.

Secrets remembrance managed to forget:
tired sailors still at sea; old squaddies scared
by snipers creeping across the carpet;
new foxholes in the asylum graveyard.

Seeing Action

They found him hanging in one of the sheds
in Ballykinler in the wounded dunes.
The fine sand wind cups into pyramids
is placed on the beach almost like cairns,

almost as if they harbour migrant souls;
reeds standing to attention, bayonets fixed.
Those bobbing targets are the heads of seals
breaking from under the surface, perplexed

at the sudden busyness of silhouettes
overhead in our strange dry world of hurt.
That traveller emptied his pockets
of nothingness right here, his last resort,

an absence without leave from desert lungs,
a drop into the planets. What happened is:
he was borne out under the fire of things,
days, words, visions, fusillades of poppies.

Icarus

What they discover – out there on the edge
of the sands, amid the armed marram grass,
sea-campion, bird's-foot and spent cartridge,
in the earth's disorder, sea's gravitas

(its many white eyes) – is that nothing sees;
the anonymous fauna too concerned
with their own delight to be witnesses.
So deaths come and go in their ungoverned

but relentless way, unhappy, unwatched
by the elements; the way that boy dropped,
out of the blue, as though he had just hatched
from the sun's nest and fallen, wet wings clipped,

already a veteran of the sky;
who might himself be that boy in fatigues
who, being washed ashore, was pulled by
strangers up the beach by his slim legs.

Fall

It used to be other people stricken
on the roadside – drunks, fainting fits, attacks –
and I'd be suggesting remedies: docken
leaves, dandelions, boor tree, old bollocks

like that, invoking the spirits of place
and custom, gods of the wayside altar,
and the ambulance, keeping a straight face.
Faith had grown vestigial, secular,

but still a defence against the unknown;
for nothing; on nothing but its own side,
the chaos of mishap and abandon.
Now it's me sprawled out like a homicide,

with bystanders leering down in a frieze
of glee at a pilgrim caught unawares
by the arc of the earth, beaten to his knees,
ready to pray; not knowing the prayers.

Obituary

Howard Scals sips a flask of red biddy
in the townland's last red telephone box.
He'll be found there, upright, by that lady
who takes her two red setters out for walks

at dawn at this crossroads where no cars cross,
before the children turn for school, before
the clean and the ordinary trespass
on old technology suddenly gone sour.

Somnolence. Humming light. A bitter grape.
This is the fox's path cut among whins,
vintage parleys no party can escape,
cigarette butts, policemen, heron cranes

– those vigilantes – on abandoned acres.
Sixty winters. An engine's rough berceuse
growls in the ditch. A votive lamp flickers.
There are no mourners waiting in the pews.

Afterwards

If any come after me in Lecale,
following the fingerprints or footsteps,
crossing the mute white water of the Quoile
which swans write on with their wings like handclaps,

into those wells feeding out like microfiche
their tiny water onto desks and roads,
they will be fishermen beached in the parish,
foreign girls in shops singing like barcodes

that elusive B-flat; librarians,
fingers buttery from scones and tray bakes,
smearing the screens, documenting the shrines
to youngsters freshly killed, plastic snowflakes;

one might be a poet with greater skill,
an eye for beauty, a subtler way
for a population distressed and unwell,
still crying out for words, to have its say.

1969

That was the summer they got in everywhere
and in numbers, not the odd specimen;
so what had hitherto been quite rare
was making broadcasts out of the bread bin

in a nasally and indistinct voice
as if the battery was running down
or the set was picking up news from space.
Bees on the turntable in the gramophone,

bunched on the floral curtains in tassels,
suspended from the coal-house roof in ropes.
That was the summer of rockets and measles
and Mr McKee's hives and giant leaps

and ghettoes in Belfast in quarantine
and falling asleep with a bee in the room,
a dead soul on the dark side of the moon,
his signals awry, a few feet from home.

Fancier

I followed behind him out to the loft.
They were at the rear of the premises,
the pigeons. We knew that, after the theft,
he'd had bolts fitted. No surprises.

The ad in the paper was 12p a word.
He was to be in the house after six
for anyone wanting to buy a bird,
so he himself would unfasten the locks.

Quick in, quick out. He had used his wife's name
but that didn't help. We knew who he was.
We didn't expect his wee girl to come
out to the back. One of those dilemmas.

I had to push past her after the shot —
one in the head. There was a skipping rope.
She was silent, white, rooted to the spot.
You want to have heard the row in the coop.

Farming

It's funny how, after a summer storm,
however powerful a single gust,
the epaulets stick to the uniform
fuchsia wears like a Chilean fascist

yet, tidying up, let your slow hand
brush ever so lightly against one stem
and there's a rain of gaudy contraband,
bloody petals as if you'd hammered them.

Some say it's a freak; on another night
there'd be carnage down to the lightest breeze
and none would notice; others that God's writ
runs gentle even to bring things to their knees;

or, I dunno, something to do with chance
or the angles of the house or nature.
I'm bored already, swearing allegiance
like a cardinal to a tin pot dictator.

Strangers

When they meet in town — migrants, the strangers —
wheeling their buggies from the new estates
built on old townlands like the Flying Horse
and Meadowlands, the mythic sobriquets

— rusting machinery in bogs, old men —
newbuilds named after places in England
(Cotswold, The Green, The Fens, The Demesne)
they behave as though it has just happened,

their exile, their loss of coordinates.
Suddenly, they are what they were before
only more so, stoic as anchorites,
making the worst of what is on offer,

sullen and mute and hugging street corners,
retreating to their old god and his cultus
of hard labour, low talk, misdemeanours,
bad luck and bad clothes. Exactly like us.

Lingua franca

As soon as they entered the house, the natives
began to speak English, that cuckoo tongue
which was in fact how they spoke among themselves
out at sea, in call centres, all along.

What welcome they gave the miraculous guest
since the bird first roosted in the roofs of their mouths,
being Irish, in what's still the Far East
of an isle annoyed by accents and bloodbaths;

inflections pulled by the magnetic waves
running to the coast of England and coal,
Liverpool, Barrow, Whitehaven – wet graves
open for seafarers, swallowing them whole.

These are no melancholic bulletins,
locally sung, but the gossip of passengers
on the one earth, a clatter of skeletons,
the most beautiful English of soldiers.

Penance [Machaon]

It was that time you were shaving my head —
tacking the clipper around the scarring
under the knap where the scalp had knitted —
my naked self in the bath, lines blurring

between love and caution: a careful task
like sewing buttons or finding a headline
and your fingertips in the heady dusk
travelling heavenward along my spine.

This is how anchorites would sit in their cells,
drunk on hunger, mortifying the flesh,
then, the story goes, be met by angels
when least expected, a tender ambush

breaking their bones, re-setting the fragments
so cleverly they were wholly renewed:
different persons from the same components,
unrecognised, harmless, misunderstood.

Forecast

Downpatrick weather. Mist over the swamp,
grey as widows' washing strung on a hedge.
When the waters rise and all hands to the pump
apply the vestiges of old knowledge

- tribal defences, jute sacks fat as pigs,
bellies bloated with sand washed from the Nile,
rank liniments against whatever plagues
breed in the mess of muck and tractor oil —

the old cosmopolis lain under brick
is roused from its medieval slumber
by simple rain. The Bargainland boutique
turns the volume up on a classic number

— by *Dawn featuring Tony Orlando* —
but already the shoppers dissipate
and coastal sun across the tundra
forces on Ardglass its own chaste climate.

Logical Investigations

I don't know how she stuck the breakdown - mine,
that is. The nerves shot like a veteran
of the Civil Service's own frontline,
all 'stress' and 'workload' as if it were Tehran.

Time off. Fresh air. Long walks by the canal
in the company of a lovely girl
(as the doctor put it, in a nutshell).
Some nut. Some girl. As if Edmund Husserl

had meant, in crying *zu den Sachen selbst*
decades before in the Scholastic class,
a bizarre Germanic brand of self-helpst,
perfect, nourishing, sweet and more like Swiss.

No ideas but in things. Believing is seeing
what is and moves and rests in her two arms:
as ecstasies, as moments of being,
as epiphanies and on her terms.

Walk

Although the sun had gone and it was black
on the narrow roads with the broken tar
around sweet Killough, and us on a break
six miles from home (like taking rooms next door),

we were safe in the crook of the lighthouse,
sending its messages over our heads
but dropping such light from its widow's cruse
to pick out berries, abandoned homesteads,

the tiny cubes a broken windscreen leaves,
maps of Alaska on a heifer's flank.
Then there were your wrists between cuffs and gloves,
old technologies glimmering like zinc,

while shipping was lost, souls still lost at sea.
Your Blackberry's glitter on the footpaths
fought for your attention and won easily,
your naked fingers plotting stars like moths.

The Downe

She is battering him around next door.
He is shouting but she keeps her mouth shut,
letting her fists do the talking; uproar
but with the signal fading in and out,

a radio play with lost dialogue
but all the necessary sound effects:
his head on the plaster after a dig,
cries when her elbow bursts his appendix;

slammed doors; his sobbing; her out in the yard,
feg smoke dancing like angels on a pin;
him calling for her, tap water run hard;
her cellphone ringtone singing *Dancing Queen*.

Moments of silence. Now there is a voice,
'mibbe you'd run me up to the Down*ee*,
don't ring the doctor, he'd get the police.'
The ambulance laughing, nee naw, naw nee.

Takabuti

There is no chance at all that she's asleep,
although the face is slack and open-lipped
as if her young man has taken a step
just now from the room and out into Egypt,

leaving her loved and in some disarray,
hollow as a gourd. Who punched her womb
right through to the walls of crispy algae,
canna seeds, stray nipples of cardamom,

has torn her heart from her and in its nest
laid language, cryptic, papery, unread,
for those who find her. Those eyes someone kissed;
eyes that stare on intimacies betrayed.

She could have been that girl dug from the dunes
exactly like that, with no hand holding hers,
but borne in penance through the avenues
awake, though murdered and on our shoulders.

Shrines

It's just as well no one pays any heed.
It lets the town ramble on as it does,
taking the lives of young men as they breed
early with young girls here in the ghettoes.

Parcels of blooms from the all-night garage
stuck to telegraph poles with Sellotape;
cellophane rattling wherever damage
is done by Stanley knife, car wreck or rope.

Hard memory. Versions of permanence
which do not work. Wayside altars to the gods,
though neglected, still are as talismans
while their old technology degrades,

the tea-lights fail for want of batteries
and the colours drain from plastic bouquets;
at their best when they grow anonymous,
denatured, despised, then stumbled across.

Foe

Downpatrick native Anwar Ibrahim
beset his friend with a samurai sword.
Another warrior and night pilgrim,
he kept that question mark in a cupboard

for one time when there was nothing to say
and no one listening. Street bravado
and something epic in the drugged affray,
something of the mythic desperado,

unshaven, at odds, in Kennedy Square,
the dead president in an upstairs flat,
when Saladin drew his scimitar
for the Lionheart and the kerchief split

by drifting gently on the razor blade.
Days punctuated by the stern tsk-tsks
of folk for whom, nonetheless, this kid
left blood drops on the street like asterisks.

Lilium

The lilies are waiting to break open,
tepals grown antique as the beaks of birds —
that rigid, that restrained and misshapen
they are husks or ghosts, torpid as lizards.

Lantern jaws tap at the windows like bone.
If dead children had drawn their slender frames,
goggle-eyed, out of the graves, and each one
with a visage sculpted from the extremes

of atrocity, we would touch their scars
in a wounded husbandry of a sort
incapable of repair or working cures.
But nothing is amiss. Those pulses smart

in there, perfect, where the planet aligns,
inside, behind chill leathery colours,
beyond the scrutiny of living things,
the anonymous virtues of flowers.

Paradise

Some shopfronts were stripped back so their past showed.
Half-words reappeared: indistinct; broken
as the same words on graves up the Killough Road.
It was unclear how those names were spoken,

let alone what was sold before they closed.
We delight to think of their good future
before the decay the workmen exposed –
how the Ankatels thought themselves secure

in the county town and were for decades;
deal-makers, lovers; by turns shy and vexed
at how the past they knew builds and degrades
each effort to reach from their world to the next

where we are, the heaven they never reached.
Such carnage in cardinal red parlours
in those last hours before the sign was switched.
That's the past. There are no survivors.

Drowning

Some boy got snagged on the lines and was pulled
in. He had been weeks revolving out there,
the sea going over every inch of his build,
emptying his pockets, ruffling his hair,

making a fuss of him for the first time
in years. The sombre men in the rib leant
over him like a drunk or a bridegroom
for he had the glaze on him of a saint,

no hoodlum or immigrant; and the bruise
on his cheek looked like the knock of an oar
or a touch from a rock when the tide rose.
He might have been a god or ancestor,

such was the care bestowed on his suffer
-ing; his pure incidence among killings
a blessing, a release; were it not for
that perfume of bath water in his lungs.

Famine

My Protestants suffered no ill-effects
of the Famine, so their skin was perfect.
Good food, holidays abroad, frequent sex
had made their parents genetically correct

so their progeny were stunning and polite,
respectful of customs, neat, good losers.
No lank bitterness from potato blight,
no styes, no cold sores and no cheap trousers,

no Fenian surliness or big red hams
the Convent girls called thighs. But though modest,
and by all accounts better in exams,
it's clear my Protestants not once noticed

that they were mine by birthright; mine to hold
shimmering in my brain as I took my pick –
as it were – ssstammering, ssstill 12 years old,
SSSilvikrin, SSSunsilk, HHHawaiian Tropic.

The Standard of Ur

Music was crushed in clay when the sky fell,
the ancients say: everything sacred
thrown down bodily with the citadel.
Nineveh, Assur, Babylon, Nimrud

reduced to alabaster and gypsum
slabs engraved with history's greatest beards
tonged by beautiful lords into blossom.
There are bald men too, probably the bards,

topless in fleeces and with plucked eyebrows.
They clutch what seem stringed instruments and play,
grateful even now for what the wind blows
in lapis lazuli and seashell inlay.

The very pose I strike when I'm allowed
in the room where she unclips her brassiere;
sharing the tribute of the same postcode
when she bows to strum a comb through her hair.

Dogs

What was removed of her after the blaze
was nothing. The view from her window held
the town below in its horrific gaze;
the privets stayed put; the paintwork still peeled

modestly – flakes of white and red and blue;
the souvenirs of the seaside still stared
up from the hearth, almost as good as new;
geraniums bloomed as if someone cared.

And the small Pomeranian bitches,
clung yapping around the smoking settee
still in love with her comforting touches
as she was brought out like Takabuti,

swathed in lint and sweet-smelling unguents,
remained accomplices after the fact
and proved that there are always innocents,
perfect in their way and somehow at fault.

Lapis Lazuli

If I keep going back to these four streets
– war for the liberation of the soil –
don't think it's to recover from defeats
(the wolf stuck with a hatchet in its skull,

the ram upright with its belly open,
hospitals burned and bulldozed, wounds red raw,
disappointment) or when crises deepen
wonderfully and without caesura.

It's more a new exhaustion borne from peace
which must be endured; this trope; the pretence
that when violence subsides there is ease
and plenty, just reward for innocence.

Two Chinamen in lapis lazuli,
behind them a third, sure his chance will come.
There will be killing: just done differently
and more slowly and by a different name.

Ponderosa

These two hands that never did a day's work.
Hoss Cartwright said you should always wear gloves
at interviews, keep your paws in the dark
to fool the barristers who trawl CVs

for hairy fingers, callouses, old hacks,
hard labour leaving teethmarks on the skin.
Brush the teeth. Shine the shoes. Leave the crucifix
on the mantelpiece. Be softly spoken.

Fair dooz. But he'd shot a man in Cyprus
or Malta, some imperial outpost
when there was no war on. A mad caprice,
maybe, a drunken jape, but at a cost:

a brief tabloid-led extravaganza,
Ulster's ironies through the narrative:
a soldier with a nickname from *Bonanza*,
tats on his knuckles reading LOVE and HAVE.

Dwelling

First it was about making the known strange
in a city barely known: the old site,
the old concepts: the Arkle Bar and Lounge,
shop fronts stripped back so their past showed, old shite,

old wells, Viking raids, Scots wounds, my father
in the Telephone Exchange putting through
one of Wingate's Chindits to another
still in Burma. Connections. A venue

for triumph as if that place was agog
like London or Paris in its own right,
with fires, gold hoards, plagues, sexual intrigue,
a human history, the works. Old shite.

Now it's a case of making the strange known:
my mother, broken-hipped, on glycerine,
attacking her toenails like a gryphon:
moon cuttings pinging off the plasma screen.

Mental

The fact is, for all the talk of custom,
tradition and rights drawn from soil and sky,
belonging and blood – that ecosystem
of precedence, something like destiny -

there is still the fox found clipped to the ditch,
all blood and snout; that boy still lost at sea,
dancing so close to the shore yet beyond reach;
the girl hanged in the shed on holiday.

Dispossessions. Lesions. The wards were called
after beaches, lakes and mountain features,
but the grounds were off-limits, nature cancelled
here as every where to which, in due course,

the wayward inmates were distributed;
leaving that warning on trees, that poem:
POISON LAID. TRESPASSERS PROSECUTED.
DOGS SHOT. Still unsettlement. Still unhome.

HISTORIES

In 1844, Hincks gave a public lecture on 'The Ancient Egyptian Language' to the Downpatrick Mechanics' Institute. This first attempt to bring the attention of the public to the language and culture of Egypt seems to have been well received by the large attendance.

Cathcart

Mesopotamia

I

To believe in 'land between two rivers' – fertile, drenched –
was easy from the brow of the Killough Road
where headstones looked out over the broad wetlands

the railway had been built upon, its clinker pathway
still on pilgrimage to the coast though the iron was long gone,
an empty scar through the rushes and reeds; the water

still mauve and stinking like the sky from oil. There was
the Ballydugan Road slithering over the marshes
with its jaded lay-by shrine where the culvert exploded

under four soldiers, the vehicle burnt as a longboat. And over
the flatlands all the way to the luxurious beach of Ballykinlar,
its imperial white leather dunes soaking up cartridges,

where squaddies toiled on the shore with four stones of lethality
in backpacks: the prickly paraphernalia of a lit-up war.
They waited dispatch to Iraq, young and tested, then as now,

to some confection of detergent and wire and fertiliser tucked
under a sleeper by a roadside, just as cap-badges and name-tags
slept in a cardboard box under the captain's bunk for the journey home.

II

The lowest point in Ireland: a foot and more below sea-level
at the Credit Union's door. In Market Street on a bad day,
it's as if the ordinary rain can call up sea dwellers from under the tarmac:

mackerel pressed against the grilles in the gutters,
a seal caught by gravity out at the tracks, coughing,
amid the cigars of reed heads; a tide-line of salt on the shoes,

the footpaths suddenly medieval and answerable to the moon.
But there is nothing miraculous here except the bare facts:
what's left of the *Hilda Parnell* is marinating on the mud flats,

arm's-lengths of black oak inflating with the water's breath,
its own ghost rocking in the sockets, tearing the grasses;
and at Tyrella, where the *Great Britain* ran into the sand –

the scale of Noah's Ark (it was said) for a year under the Mournes –
those are bullets (.22, .50, .303) outstripping the dunes,
nosing into clear water, blooming in the deep gravel as anemones.

So many monsters in a small place, just under the surface,
and none of them maleficent as such, but unreflective, inert,
taking bearings and purpose from each disturbance of the local heart.

III

Flight Into Egypt, JMW Turner, Ulster Museum

Yes, the eye is drawn to the vast centre of the painting,
as with the others of its period. The eternity of light,
the blue heaven. The snake, of course, the serpent,

black and sinewy and watchful and rising as if to strike,
vivid and menacing and as memorable as devils always are,
impressing itself upon the eye as perhaps the one defined, crisp,

eloquent dweller of this evasive and ungainly coastline.
That snake, those rocks, this sand of the desert.
But struck too by those hunched figures at large,

the woman and her child barely discernible on the cliff top,
on the donkey which, however frail and spindly, mounts
a worthy resistance to the quite wild figure of Joseph,

striding up and out into Ulster. There is certainly the idea of fleeing,
being put to flight – the condition of the fugitive and not just the innocent.
I can think now of the population that descended on the barony

in the 70s, on the run from the city wards of Lenadoon and Turf Lodge,
a colony of strangers descending on the outskirts, locals bristling in the bars,
then going home to lock their doors against people like themselves.

IV

How wonderful. For a moment along the River Quoile the beeches
are so big in autumn, so blown, they are like high-rise buildings
with all the lights on; for a moment they are nothing of nature

but are all interior – flock, concealed lamps, lush furnishings.
In New Orleans, after the hurricane, the waters had risen
so high and brought so much with them along the streets,

belongings were nesting in the tree-tops: suitcases, underwear,
pillows, TV sets, armchairs: what couldn't be nailed down
picked up by the armful and settled perfectly on the boughs.

Whole lives, in other words. Whole histories. Emptied graves.
Down here by Steamboat Quay, the bodies drifting by are swans,
a peloton of busy, silent feet, pacing currents from the open sea,

and yellow toadstools of the foam turned up by the floodgates.
Whether to tree or gradient or home, the waters will make their way
to whatever level suits the season's mood. We'll not stop it now.

Dulse fingers on glass in the phonebox's aquarium.
Now is the time to build a ship for tomorrow — of gopher wood,
if such is to be found: 300 cubits long, 50 wide, 30 cubits high.

On The Inscriptions at Van

It took Hincks nearly a year to assimilate the riches revealed to him, and him alone, in the Van inscriptions of Schulz ... Of all Hincks's reports, this is probably the single most important one... It opens though with this statement: I wish to enable my readers to judge for themselves as to the correctness of my conclusions, but I do not consider it either necessary or expedient that they should travel to them by the same path which I took myself ...

Daniels

When he thinks of the noise it makes, their speech,
it must be as the sound mud makes in the sun
travelling from wet decay to the singing clinker
carrying these incisions of pitch and emphasis,
each mark a ghost of sound, as an ammonite
is the ghost of an ammonite curled up in the Flood.
Or is something. Or is nothing.
Delicate noises signifying much or little,
far back, guttural, buried, the clack-clack of insects
breathing like miners below lapis lazuli walls,
bolting on their armour plate in secret,
the tiny mandibles of the ant-lion in wait
for *a city to become heaps, a dwellingplace*
for dragons, and an hissing.

I prefer conducting them by the shortest route to the point which I reached circuitously, and after frequently retracing my steps.

Outside, the sodden earth subsides
another inch on where his people lie
below ground but above the village still,
gathering around the ramparts of his God,
defeated by Him. Wind and sea and salt
cut lumps from the anonymous slabs they raise.
In dreams, it is the sound of their tongues clanging
like bronze doors, like bells. Like bronze.

In 1846, an Irish clergyman named Edward Hincks, was able to read the name of King Nebuchadnezzar(II) and his father, on clay bricks that travelers had brought back from Mesopotamia. This both confirmed the existence of this person noted in the book of Daniel, and his claim to be a great builder of Babylon.

Younker

And he himself is aware already
that in there, somewhere, among what's written down,
though every noise the antique jaws release
rolling inside the sand, inside the very nation,
is maddening, impossible, unnerving, arch,
like wind creaking in the buried masts on Ararat,
like the discourse of famine beetles yet some few miles off,
though someone must have spoken something,
cried out something of joy or tedium or despair,
there was as well a listener. Who, improbably, understood.

*

Hincks had been present at the unrolling of the mummies in the museum of the society on 17 & 18 October 1850
Northern Whig 19 October 1850

When the Museum unwrapped them,
the mummies, I was staring
not at the past as such
but on the face of disease:

blackened, disfigured,
bodies of tar.
One of them torn
apart by the bandages;

the other imperfect,
lazy-eyed, twisted,
but nonetheless real.
This hand touched hers.

For all her enchantments,
her name and her prayers
and disappointing tattoos,
like some drowned sailor,

I might have seen her,
bony and wasted,
her womb and heart raided,
in the Down Infirmary.

How Dr Hincks succeeded in sinking his first shaft, I hardly understand - but sunk it he certainly
has, and unless I look about me, he will anticipate all I have to say on the subject.

Col Rawlinson to Renouard, 27 Oct 1846

*

Even now the horror of it is.

Plain talk does not alter it:
Casualty. Accident and Emergency.
A side room lit by aluminium chalices.

It is orderly and clean like a kitchen
and full of women seeing to wounds and sores.
In the darkest of humours, the knives are grinning.
The inner chambers each hold the stricken selves.

A nurse's wrist is trickling a tattoo.
Fingers, holding a dish to my father's chin,
wear signs of other lives – a ring,
a blackened nail, small stigmata.

In Nineveh, or what they took for Nineveh,
they found a copper cauldron near the bodies
and goblets from which they may have drunk
a sedative or poison. Everything rendered
to an explanation that makes no sense at all.

It seems that Hincks kept Norris abreast of his progress and that Norris communicated to Rawlinson in Baghdad what Hincks was up to.

Daniels

*

Such an impertinence to adopt his voice
who might more easily have anticipated mine
had he set his antennae thus and thus,

detecting inflections from the grand design
of utterance not yet made, words not yet acts.
Less breaches us than English and German.

And this is to understand that writing connects
sound and song and thought through time
and it marches over the leaves like so many insects,

unclassified as yet, as yet unread and not at home,
still fashioning itself as at Belshazzar's feast,
strange characters crawling across history like the genome,

a sense already there already, waiting to be released.

Time after time, Rawlinson's friends asked him to make a definitive statement about the way in which he obtained the values in his Syllabary; and his answer to them was always the same, "I have no idea how I arrived at them".

E A Wallis Budge, The Rise and Progress of Assyriology, 1925

*

It was something to look in her blind eyes,
wide-open, flicking the dark from point to point.
Each morning led to the chair two-double,
arms outstretched, manoeuvred round door frames

like a wheelbarrow stacked with cardigans and love.
Propped up, she was her own monument, barely human:
lion-headed, bull-bodied, talking (if at all)
in riddles; toenails epic, rattling on the linoleum.

My great unmarried grandmother, breaching her time.
She was warm from herself like bread and smelled of butter.
Still muscular, bearded, afflicted like Maeve of Connacht:
there was a bed sore you might put your fist in.

Sometimes at evening she would howl in distress:
coming through the walls the noise another century makes.
A child who craved her papery hands might creep up on her,
ducking the oyster eyes. "I know you're there," she said.

*

Although Henry Rawlinson made the initial attempt at translating the 210 lines on the Black Obelisk in 1850, he
missed some critical readings ... Hincks argued that 'Yua, mar Humri, was none other than Jehu, son of
[the house of] Omri. Jehu, of course, was the king of Israel known for his aggressive chariot driving (2 Kings 9:20).

Younker

Victorian entirely, the work. Rebellious, somewhat.
Picking through the detritus of an empire entirely gone,
a failure to be moved by grandeur or its decay,

or to achieve a sense of superiority by being alive,
thriving, and still rolling a red carpet across the planet
for civil servants to stroll upon under parasols.

Like must engage with like. Whatever about the discovery
of possible polyphony, the syllabic nature of the characters
or the name of Jehu, son of Omri, on the Black Obelisk,

missed by everyone, this was your great victory, Dr Hincks:
"It is evidently not considered desirable that an Irishman
should have the opportunity of making any discoveries."

Put that in your Turkish pipe, Colonel, and draw on it.
In short, identifying with the plunderers alive nor dead.
Unlike the hoarders of the British Museum,

stacking the rubble against the walls of the Empire
to strengthen them; and the wily scholars across Europe
for whom breaking the language was an act of war

successfully embarked upon – just loving the talk of kings,
courts, courtiers, conquests, the familiar extreme bombast
of monsters, getting one over on, really, the Sultan, Kaiser and Tsar,

those Janissaries, those Cossacks, those Hussars, those tribes
falling upon Lebanon, cutting populations to the very bone –
by reading them. And understanding only too damn well.

On 7 June 1854, the day after the British Museum had paid Hincks 'for the amount agreed by the Trustees to be
paid to you upon the completion of your engagement', Sir Henry Ellis wrote to Rawlinson about Hincks's
manuscripts, inviting him to inspect them and even offering to send him a copy of them.

Cathcart

Melancholy Suicide at the Downpatrick Asylum

'On Monday, at twelve o'clock, Dr R C Clarke JP (coroner), held an inquest in the Board-room of the above institution on the body of a young woman, named Margaret Gordon, who was about twenty-four years of age, a patient in the Asylum, who committed suicide on the previous evening by drowning herself in a pond of water in the grounds.'

Down Recorder, 31 July 1886

I

After the drowning, after they had fished the pond with a pole
"having a hook on it", and hauled her out with anklets of weed,
her petticoat sodden, the first lift took her as far as the boiler-room
where distressed staff thought the heat would restore her.

It must have been an unremarkable summer — it was July
but the furnace was burning and the waters still deep,
though clearly the woman, being tall, had gone down
to the waters and lain her body down in them.

"She had taken the deceased inside of the railing
and she just came as far as the little gate with her
when she made a rush back again to the water."
It had happened so quickly. She had moved so quickly

from the nurse to the pond that no one could reach her,
though the nurse had gone in and strong men behind her.
They worked for hours in the boiler-room on her
but nothing amid kindling, iron piping or panic

was any use to her. As a last resort, they sent to the house
for an electric battery and applied it to her. It is 1886.
It failed. Already the Home Rule Bill had fallen
and militia as usual had run amok in Downpatrick

and someone somewhere was plotting unrest
of an old-fashioned nature – agrarian violence,
gunshots in the grading yard, unpopular and futile.
The inquest recommended the pond be walled in.

II

Surely that pond had lain for years in wait,
the perfect partner for her peculiar want.
Things do not happen. They too discriminate:

the knife in the linen drawer; the open vent
through which a sheet is knotted for a noose;
the bullet in the pistol idly lent.

Things arrange themselves to pay their dues.
So for you, Margaret Gordon, that July
when you knew you had nothing else to lose

but your anger; which weighed so heavily
you had to kneel to rinse your lungs of air.
The waters met your diligence half-way.

And that is how places and objects cohere
with how we move each day from dawn to dawn.
You'd have lived if you'd have lived elsewhere

but everything is inevitable once it's done.

A deep mystery hangs over Assyria, Babylonia and Chaldea. With these names are linked great nations and great cities dimly shadowed forth in history; mighty ruins, in the midst of deserts, defying, by their very desolation and lack of definite form, the description of the traveller; the remnants of mighty races still roving over the land; the fulfilling and fulfilment of prophecies … desolation meets desolation: a feeling of awe succeeds to wonder; for there is nothing to relieve the mind, to lead to hope or to tell
of what has gone by.

from *Nineveh and its Remains, a narrative of an expedition to Assyria during the years 1845, 1846 and 1847*
Austen Henry Layard (John Murray:1867)

On The Khorsabad Inscriptions

I look upon Dr Hincks as the true first discoverer of the Assyrian language
William Henry Fox Talbot, 1861, letter to Julius Oppert

Meanwhile, she bore the girl on her own back for three days those six miles.
Will it be believed? On Dundrum strand, the *Great Britain* is still on its side,
a palace of cables and masts and pianos and perishable goods,

a colossal wreck, an empire ploughed back into the sand. After eight months,
the novelty of the impossible having already taken place is wearing thin,
for all Brunel himself had come, his fat cigar smoking and his top hat like a fat cigar,

another dwarf among the monsters famine let loose among the dunes
to stare and beg and disappoint like Egyptians and Persians and Greeks of that age,
stupid among monuments, knowing neither who built them nor how they spoke.

Of course, as soon as they reached the infirmary, her daughter died.
Of disease. Of rust on the skin. Of a tongue big as a gourd.
Meanwhile, in Killyleagh the stern Assyrian surgeons relentlessly advance

over the sheets in the Rector's study now his ladies have left (rock cakes on lace).
Their clay headdresses are as square and stiff as sails or their own grey faces.
A gaze fixed still on the disc of the sun as flat as earth, nothing turns their heads or his.

Certainly not suffering. Certainly not that tableau of two women carved into the moment,
concubines, perhaps, unfortunates of a warrior nation. And so is lost forever
what he is searching for, among the tiny skeletons the words of a language leave,

among the bird's-feet scamperings, among the marks a dove might leave
lighting on mud-flats when waters subside. Something beached like death itself.
Something massive. Overbearing. Irresistibly finite. A determinative. An adverb. An ark.

England

When my father appears now he is surrounded by sails
though he never was at sea. They are headstones, I think; grey canvas
lifted to the wind by the dead from the hollow boat of the planet,

for which tacking the trolley to Coronary to end his travels
was an education in the wherewithal of caves and alcoves,
where memory begins with that low throaty origin the clarinet

owns at the outset of air, a wonder among bright useless utensils:
then the screaming of wheels, the stopping of the airwaves,
his deathbed singing more guttural, more foreign, each minute.

*

In every direction, the honeysuckle's strung along the long acres,
among the blackberry and whitethorn, among the goosegabs.
My father still insists that's the woodbine, although he's six years dead

and I think now as then of that shop on Scotch Street, where smokers
were peddled Craven A, 'for your throat's sake'. They went off like squibs.
But the tightness in his chest - the spittle that bunched like black thread

in the sink when he raked it up each morning - was paraffin. Scars
on his lungs he feared was cancer when they showed as cobwebs
on the X-Rays. Hobnails clattered away in free fall when his boots rotted.

*

We came on a sheep that had fallen into the ditch, its wool soaked
so to its back it would drown like a man in two inches of rot water.
Such a beast is not persuaded. He had to kneel on its belly,

into the very bog of an animal, to wring it by the two horns till it hooked,
its screaming mouth in his own, its aria. He took it like a predator
without a thought, the two wrestling in the drain and roaring *a capella*

till he pulled it back on board. I watched it cross the field, shocked
by maggots alive on the butcher's apron of its red, white and blue rear
like a honeycomb they were eating, yet it with the new step of a gazelle.

*

Though the clasp of the faux leather box of skeletal remains was electroplated,
inside it was all real: the scarlet plush flesh where the clarinet was interred
in its parts like a concealed weapon. Barrel, bore, cylinder, ligature,

for assembly tongue-and-groove till the tip rail took the slim wafer of the reed.
That hollow organism – ebonite, mpingo – intricate vertebrae dismembered,
struck the squaddies arresting his rebel son in their damp khaki couture,

leaving him wheezing and suddenly old in the hall, as also to be tested and tried,
elements forced together until they whistled. Then discarded, broken. Not referred
to again until this moment and this narrative of it which has something of caricature.

*

It was all about Raffles and Wooster and Terry-Thomas and Mainwaring's moustache,
and the way the British outmarched the Yanks heading out to the aerodrome,
stamping up the middle of the street while the homeboys took it as sport,

precision of parade ground ceremonies; shellac discs of Heddle Nash,
the only English tenor, or any other than the Count, to be given houseroom;
the Band of the Irish Guards - a letter from Colonel Jaeger something of a passport

to a version of Albion, though as much use when visiting the barbed wire of Long Kesh,
as Colman's mustard or Peter England shirts. What strange Stockholm syndrome,
that stuff. That nonsense. Lending to an accident the testing loyalty of the convert.

*

This is England, my England. Or his. Or ours. And this is how he gave voice
to it, ferrying oil from the back gate of Castle Ward to the townland of Bright
where the countryside was fashioned to resemble the wheaten and soda

landscapes he'd seen his first time from the plane as an apprentice
heading on union work to Loughborough. And even then, he was back on site
noting parts for the wee band in the Triumphal March & Chorus from *Aida,*

in memory of Bernard, his uncle, choked in a flue in Barrow on methane gas
in Nineteen Eighteen and never recovered, so though there is a lump of granite
there's nary a relic even as odd as Oliver Plunkett's skull in Drogheda.

*

There was a bomb in the bandstand. No one expected it. It was the second attack.
All day reports marvelled at how musicians could be slaughtered so casually,
horses stuck through with nails, the liquorice sticks broken and scattered,

notes never to be picked up, the many injured; epic action with its own soundtrack.
Summer in the heartlands. The ragwort proliferating on the same roadsides lazily
where tinkers were burnt out by locals, leaving tarmac scorched and cratered.

I think of his death by suffocation, by drowning as surely as if by shipwreck;
of that figurine from Ur of a ram scared in a thorn bush in gold and lapis lazuli
in the British Museum. Of his weeping that day as if it mattered.

On The Third Persepolitan Writing

Major Rawlinson ... is very anxiously looking for something from you respecting the Babylonian inscriptions ...
You may be gratified to learn that he says 'Dr Hincks is in the right track and I look with much interest at anything
from him'.

Renouard, 1846

It is strange to think of it as immersion –
given the clay tablets, fresh from the oven,
given the sowing with saltpetre of subjugated fields,
given the reckless irrigation over centuries
and the consequent seeding of the homeland with salt –

but still it is irresistible as a metaphor
of what is needed to go down into language,
vulnerable, naked, raw, without apparatus,
time and again going under to rescue it,
each time searching for what you are searching with.

The lungs, the lips, the teeth, the tongue, the brains,
waterlogged with talk, chambers flooding with grammar,
the old wineskin of the body fit to burst.
Water is everywhere, after all, between rivers,
dry land a hyphen and mud a half-way house.

When a body is washed ashore after months
(the organs ringing, skin bright-coloured as a map,
a simple life suddenly made notable and distinct,
an object of awe as once, perhaps, of worship,
spectacular, carven, teak, the eyes still azure blue)

the tail of his wet gown fistles on the study door, whispering.

I am very sure that there is a strong feeling in some influential quarters that I must be kept out of the field
of discovery, whatever may occupy it. I am now laid on the shelf; and I never expect to have again the means of
pursuing my discoveries.

Edward Hincks, Killyleagh, 1856

In his delirium my father,
who had stopped singing, sang.
> *South of the border*
> *down Mexico way ...*
But recalled nothing of it
afterwards, returned to himself.

But there was the evidence of the white line
wriggling on the green monitor
and aluminium tingling on the bedside table
and water lapping in the plastic beaker.
And the thin walls of Coronary Care
throbbing like pigskin when the sound went up.

They will allow the use of it privately to some of their present employees, so as to enable him to carry on the work – I being cast off ... Rawlinson will be in London, I suppose, forthwith. He was expected before this. And I have no doubt that he will be allowed free access to all that the Museum possesses.

Hincks: letter,1854

There was present an unconscionable mood,
illegible, dun-coloured, hard-core,
something ignorant and dull in store
at all times and at every turn of the road.

The curve of the coast below his house
caught bodies washed up in the tide –
fishermen swept over the side;
children plucked from the shore without fuss,

played with a while, then thrown back;
riper souls who cast their own selves in
bemused by disease or the crippling sun.
Unsavoury baptisms, florid and maverick.

Rawlinson missed the most exciting aspect of the monument: the first known mention of a Hebrew king, of any biblical phenomenon, in an ancient record. It was none other than Edward Hincks (again) who identified Jehu, son of Omri, as named and depicted bringing tribute to Shalmaneser.

Daniels

On Dundrum strand,
the *Great Britain* is still on its side,
a palace of pianos and perishable goods.
A few yards off from the famine beaches,
is an empire ploughed back into the sand,

a colossal wreck. At the coastguard watch-house,
where the great ship struck,
to this very day they are gathering coal
from the Yorkshire tunnels.
It rolls ashore like loaves of black bread.

The tribute of Jehu (Ia-ú-a), son of Omri (Hu-um-ri); I received from him silver, gold, a golden saplu-bowl, a golden
vase with pointed bottom, golden tumblers, golden buckets, tin, a staff for a king, (and) wooden puruhtu.

                                                                    from the Black Obelisk

The dresser the squaddies fell against in the Crescent
spilled Belleek vases on the cardinal red tiles,
ballerinas, ill-painted figurines from Bray,

fruit bowls and dogs with stern faces.
A white and blue and speckled store.
My mother was on her hunkers for days

amid the ringing debris, re-fashioning
grotesques with glue: humpbacked, eyeless,
two-faced goddesses with angels' wings.

Given time, you might reconstruct everything
a lifetime of habit from discarded things:
the bird-song of china, her sobbing.

I did, though, add a sentence in the paperback edition (page 332) just to show its context, before
others are misled into thinking that Rawlinson's many years of decipherment work depended on Hincks.

                                                                    adkinsarchaeology.com

Let me make it clear. His cult endures.
But Old Persian was already undone.
The Elamite tongue he despised so much
he left it to his crony Norris.
And 'Babylonian' or 'Assyrian'
or 'Akkadian', whatever, was mine.
                    And he stole it.

Already I had stumbled on
the insight of our Irish condition.
What we were for; how unfit we were
to speak for the Empire.
Better always an imperial dilettante
to fly the flag than a humble scholar:
                    eccentric, curt,

remote, marginal, rural and Irish.
Simply by being myself, I saw –
was blinded by it; complete,
all of a piece and at once –
the whole relation between the islands.
I had uttered the very words myself,
                    laugh as you will:

"having had the misfortune to be born in Ireland"
and "not on the favoured side of the channel".
Phrases the Major could no more unpick
than he could the Third Persepolitan Writing
without my conclusions. Against my will,
I am a rebel, thus, like Young Ireland:
                    equally risible and crushed.

Holding the cure of souls in the parish, I cannot allow a curate to take my place, who would give
instructions to my parishioners of a different character from what I have myself given.

                                                        Hincks, letter, Killyleigh, 1852

He would visit my father,
       Reverend Hincks,
on his way from bed to bed.
       Imagine waking
to that black obelisk,
       still and relentless,
scarred and disturbed, but of Heaven,
       turned up by design
amid the coughing and the pain.
       The desperation.
A weathered and weathering gaze
       upon transience,
on the solemn wearing away
       of what wears away:
the flesh. And only the sternness of it,
       its seriousness
(like a landslide on tablets of clay)
       pulls him up short.
Then would he read on the clipboard
       the clamped pink sheets
and, with time and ineffable patience,
       understand what they say.

SURVIVALS

"They have all a great reverence for burial-grounds, which they sometimes call by the name of 'Cities of the Silent', and which they people with the ghosts of the departed, who sit each at the head of his own grave, invisible to mortal eyes"

from *An Account of the Kingdom of Caubul* (1815) by Mountstuart Elphinstone,

quoted in *Lalla Rookh* (1817) by Thomas Moore

Silage

It was a bad year, the annals say, if in winter
you could see to the back wall of the shed:
elemental debris when the cattle feed ran out,

cobwebs splayed out like skin off the black beams
(those dead wings of the fields disturbed and opening),
the black beams visible for the first maybe in decades,

the concave ribcage of a willow basket still brooding
and down there, in the shadow, what might be a man –
fugitive shoulders hunched against unaccustomed light –

but is in fact a greatcoat: ghosting, doused in slurry
a dozen summers before, the scrim spoiled by oil
or an arm caught in a harvester, torn beyond repair,

a write-off ripening for this accidental burial.
How it recovered. A child wandered among workers
leaning like veterans on grapes and pitchforks,

caught in a frieze of sour dust, the brittle light.
Death hadn't happened yet though on its way down years
towards him: its features, its fusty knap and chill,

the sudden drainage of character and love
from the build of the familiar; evacuation, remains
but pure absence *in extremis*. Innocence urged to darkness –

'See what he has in his pockets, young fella!' –
where the big figure still loomed, blinded, hollowed out,
kneeling on what was left of the bales as if tired or wounded.

And each good day since, that shy visage rebuilt thread by thread —
tilt of a forehead, a lank collar shrouding the outline of a jaw:
night-patrolling, diesel-fuelled, on-the-run outlaw,

haunter of broad daylight entering in by strange gaps,
some shell-shocked inmate, an old ally with soldier's heart
but already braved. From the dry cavity of the body, deftly drawn,

slivers of blue egg-shell in the boy's palm, a small bird flown.

INJURIES

I

Flaubert in Egypt

I only turned round and the season had changed: it was autumn
and the shadows of clouds were climbing the hill with backpacks laden

though a moment before they had been light of foot when they were young
and used to crossing the flatlands with white skin and without effort.

Or it was suddenly night-time, dampness, and those were bats' wings
across the eyes, or webs a spider had been spinning since morning

from the hedge to the bay tree, as if it were throwing its doily over a gap
as broad and as treacherous as a falls. The dunes where there had been roads

were silent and the mist drifted over them, so drained and inconsolable
I was compelled to understand them with raw palms like a scholar:

I go dreaming into the future, where I see nothing, nothing, but days spent
shooting stray dogs in a Cairo dump, dishonest bakers nailed up by the ears.

It was as if suddenly I was acquainted with cattle, awaiting their visits
to the iron gate sprinkled with slabber, or dragging the salt lick's smooth

gypsum catafalque right up to the centre of their solemn conclave,
to the measured appraisal of their considerate eyes. They know the indifference

of all things – to all things – in blocks of ice or bales, dead calves, foxglove
or ringworm, rainfall or farmer – and appreciated it with rare sophistication

and no alarm at all, an adequate comportment, a version of love, a presence.
They stand for the Earth, being attentive. How they mustered, for example,

around the *Hilda Parnell* – or what's left of her on the riverbank, carcass bone dry,
dismembered – stepping between the charred beams like flamingos or ballerinas,

so much not touching the sides, not causing a flake to fall or a splinter,
they might have been cargo, left standing organic and mute for years after the wreck,

though tethers adrift, while the boat rotted under them. I only turned round
and was exiled from the world of remembering without worry or regret,

away from the burden of imagining things and instead submitting to their blows,
awash without hurt, struck by forgetting, caught by the planet and on my own two knees.

II
Impact

What you see first is your own blood on the ground and the second
is that, though it is thicker than water, it is closer to water than oil

and so red only the blue of the sky or the sea could be more blue;
then that drops of it splash in starry geometries, asterisks

on paving stones and, when you shake your head, it's a rainfall
on shirtsleeves, on the cuffs, on the backs of your hands, on concrete,

so many small doilies stitching themselves into a crocheted antimacassar.
This in the course of what seems to be an hour, but isn't, becomes a liquid

with no beginning or end, just margins and those fluid and exchanging.
There is a sense of your own self and its capacity for being wounded,

your generosity towards exposure, towards menace and affliction,
your open-handed and open-hearted hospitality to those sojourners;

an abstract concept observed under way, at work in close conditions.
It is one's own self and it is going to die like this, certainly, relentlessly,

but not yet. Broken spectacles. A wet cap which one must don again
though everything is so obviously amiss. How much one just wishes to sleep

and how soon one will be able to, if one should consider it as such,
as that young man did, your brother, who had such bad nights

even on the good nights, that, when it came to considering death,
that state of consideration, he relished the concept of the depth of that rest.

III
Care

In the heart ward of the new hospital your father didn't live to make it to,
you are wired up with sensors at the same coordinates on almost the same torso

and this is the constellation of Orion – nipples, underarm, shoulders, belly –
taking shape on your chest as many times on his, sketched out in cable,

and you are waiting to die like him. That will be like being picked up bodily,
– a meaning of rapture – and the only warning will be an unbalancing; unsteadily

hoisted into a warm darkness where there is no resistance to what is not a defeat
though it is the beginning of a journey only part of which you will complete.

This nurse was on duty the night he died she's sure (was it so recent or that long ago?)
and she recalls during the attack his strange song behind the screens. Mute and agog,

the narrative of your own days is right now played out in another context
which gives bearings to your own – admissions, discharges, reference notes, text –

reaching back four generations to other collapses, more suddenness, stark rescues
and starker losses against the odds when, even with all the accoutrements of success

present and at work and with no deficits, there was nonetheless the miracle of death.
In this way, your body is close to the bodies of men you never met, tight as a wreath,

so tight their pipe smoke clings. These are the facts. There is nothing peculiar.
The archives show where the arteries harden, where the valves misfire

across incarnations of sinew and bone. It is readable and predictable, this narrative
consists of the weaknesses of the organism you call your own, with which you live.

It is a tale told by others. Isn't the wonder of a story that it is told and so exceeds
its prophet in every regard, because it is heard? And isn't this what the creeds

mean by immortality — what else? — a breach opened in time's thickness,
through which what's personal vanishes and where blood rushes

in, anonymous, disinterested, relentless, perfect and breathtakingly intimate?
The channels are suffering. Welcome to their wounds, their terminals, their vomit.

In Coronary Care, the lights are low and it's always autumn — singing monitors,
dried blood, strange bruising, internal organs made visible by the firelight of stars.

The land where your fathers died, among natives who found them on the beach
and did their best. So this shoreline of coarse linen is as familiar as their speech —

each organism has this history of death — but it is circumstance, this tale, these flakes
of the remarkable that give the soliloquy of this bloodied shirt something of heroics

that are only partly yours, belonging also to others, which is the miracle
of human lives. Not only does one not control the tale that one might tell

of others but even one's own remains one version of events, one soundbite;
privileged because one's own, but neither exclusive nor the more accurate.

There are others for whom it matters that an erasure occurs, however clinical,
and for whom, surprisingly, it is not as an aside and nor is it completely whole.

IV
Patient

Not having been given to thinking about things under much,
the tiny old lady opposite in her floral winceyette nightdress
who is pressing the buzzer for the nurse and wondering

why the light isn't dimming, the light over her bed and who
is calling out about such failure of promises through the night,
struck me as, in fact, a meditation. And though she isn't the one

who's been sneezing like a contraption invented to mimic
human sneezes by copying a one-off whooping like the call
of a water bird and repeating it, note for note, over 40 iterations,

give or take, and doing it at 35-minute intervals so memorably
that nurses come from other wards with their patients in tow,
those capable of moving, to join in with a song that is all chorus,

she collates that virtue also in herself, her small being
coming to grips with the amazing trickery of remote access
from a townland homestead to a hospital glamorous as a liner.

It brings to mind that heifer whose back was broken
in two by the ministrations of the bull, no fault of his
or hers, no pause in the technology at work, no default

position, absolutely nothing even remotely like regret,
lying prone in the byre, kicking what seemed like her many heels,
howling from deep in her misshapen belly, though, howling,

howling, with the brand of noise dishevelled wind instruments
might make, dinged trumpets, saxophones bright as her maimed spine
and as visible, with the notes of an oboe and clarinet at play also,

because the organs of this universe demand some orchestrations
which can be interpreted as railing about the facts of things –
how they also go wrong without trace, how they equally transcend

muck and blood – and though misconstrued the demand, though inaccurate
the reading, misplaced the apportionment of sensibility, unwise the thought,
O how she kicked, and even when the kicking stopped, sang out against the stars.

V
Wards

Imagine a place where they're stored, by design not accident;
omit those damaged by a known, human assailant –

though even that cause on occasion has been ascribed to the stars,
vapours on the moon, a sudden eclipse, a fall of meteors;

and think of the carnage wrought by the pure stuff of things,
nothing else; how we gather it to ourselves, as holdings,

belongings, our goods we cherish and think stolen or earned
or derived from misfortune; obstacles overcome or mourned.

What it does, though – the planet – is simply progress
its business along the circuit of what we call space

but which is, in fact, a thing; predictable, a kind of solid
with dimensions, character and edges. What we do is collide

with it periodically to more or less deadly effect.
Bed after bed, the wards pay tribute to the impact:

the gentleman in the camelhair coat left red raw
head to toe after an assault from the aurorae;

that battered old lady the sun's corona took against
in her own backyard, a shocking bowed head red-rinsed,

blots on the pillow; the boy whose face gravity ground
so well into the tarmac it was as if its only errand

was to drive this very point home but leave him still alive;
those others; these; but always only those who survive.

VI
Gravity

The universe is getting its own back for every step I take within it,
a literal recovery. What else could it be? Gravity holds things to the planet

and doesn't let go and every day pulls back with more or less force.
It happens this blood on the concrete is what happens with more force.

In these minutes left to me, I undertake a study of things. My spectacles,
lenses rose-tinted with it; the glittering cellphone, skin like a mackerel's;

that pen in the flower bed; bright sunlight warm on the back of my head;
the many perfect engines of bees in the canopy, ignorant and unafraid.

Consideration must be given to the orbit of the Earth. This is not about pain
but about impact; being struck and re-struck; restored suddenly to the profane

legislation of a thing. Blood for Atticus Finch was the paying of a tribute:
We could see him shiver like a horse shedding flies; his jaw opened and shut;

he was alist, but he was being pulled gradually toward us. There is no malice
or intent of any kind. But there is collison and there is still hurt, that surplus

of understanding by which it is known there is a human. In Egypt, Flaubert
shot stray dogs at the aqueduct Cairenes used as a dump; a slaughter

completely random, anonymous and forgotten except as an illustrative aside
and only for what it says occurs when power and art and poverty coincide:

small cruelty of a kind again, but itself as an aside and difficult to assign
to the wilfulness of one soul. It is the whole circumstance, rather; a doctrine

of this very desert and its nomad lives, the Earth's dispensables. A stone's throw
off stands the monument to the young man shot by police, his concrete barrow

a reliquary of old thought, a vat of nothing but grief and, when that's exhausted,
a curio, a solid anomaly in marshy ground, a story in which few are interested,

and itself adjacent to the new cinema, fingers of light already moving on its wall.
There is of course the damage wrought by oneself, physical and moral,

but there is also this silence in which blows are sustained. On all fours,
hit by a rock flung by the sun, I am coming to grips again with the contours

of a way to travel. *There is the stench of flesh rotting,* and from those rogues
on the dump, their indifferent complaint, *the gnawing and belching of dogs.*

Kelp

'Then, from the sunless depths, came other images no one had expected ... there, clearly visible, were the bodies of some of the 228 passengers who perished when flight AF447 plunged into the sea, several still strapped into their seats.' The Guardian, 4 April 2011

When something almost human washed ashore,
firesides rehearsed the old ontology:
the very dead themselves, not just their souls;
fleshly still because they were close to earth;
changed by water; inhabited by it
so long the bones were soft, the skin transformed
so their own loved ones wouldn't know them now.

And though they are down there, buried under,
is not to say they do not want the sky,
clutching at swimmers' ankles lazily,
as confident as lovers, louche as drunks,
the drowned ballast of thallus, stipe, holdfast,
hankering for the poetry of air.

But dragged in from the sea, unbuttoned, torn,
they would be satin wedding gowns gone off,
mermaids' petticoats sloughed off by the breeze,
ribbons and bows from dead girls still out there.
Harvested, they would be a fabric –
the missing – strung on hedges by the beach

till their tongues are dry. And for all their use
dug in to the alien corn, boiled down
for the marrow, their clipped wings the dead weight
of saddlebags once lifted from the salt,
ground down for fixatives, toothpaste, gum,
erased from the records of the marine,

still each time some other one goes under
– a planeful pulled from the air, or that boy
waltzed along the gravel beds for weeks
and washed up changed at an altar of tea-lights,
or the girl gone off-road at a bad bend
found pressed to the windscreen like a starfish

– our slick angels down there lean closer in.
Tall dames in flight like nuns, leathery men
armed with bladders: what rough ceremony
of parasols and sodden picnic linen
in liturgies of love on the wet lawns,
with attar of salad dressing and ice cream.

Losing Mary Travers

Mary Travers was a teacher who was shot dead on 8 April 1984 by gunmen who were trying to kill her father Tom Travers, a magistrate. She was 22.

I

The light wind in the boiling trees
has such fine hair. This countryside –
Eglantine, Windsor, Adelaide,
Derryvolgie's mountain loanen
carved with a shock through city brick.
Even the thug has farmers' hands.

There is nothing ordinary.
What happens when it happens shows
the strangeness that would stay concealed:
nestling tumour, sudden cure,
the weakest with the weight of grief,
a hare against the blazing whins.

II

Who was that staring in at the window
of the café where you sat with your dad?
Merciless teasing. *You have an admirer.*

III

Sticking to facts makes no more sense:
cuneiform on Hincks's desk.
Cool endeavours; calm precision
of the wonderful eking out
unlikely joys like a hedgehog.
Democracy: that history
against which is put up the heart,
tiny, unprofitable, plain,
wholly bothersome and exposed.
Always its bird's-foot scampering.

IV

I heard the shots,
a Sunday dead,
three streets away.

In Eglantine
the air was still,
birds went tumbling

into the clouds
as what broke out
across the roofs –

that intimate,
brash, echoing,
unexpected,

that brief and wrong –
was confetti,
was like applause.

V

There is no going on or back.
Forgetfulness is everywhere.
The cold stone by the sea is salt.

It happens we are buying trees,
my bride and I: silver birches,
rowan, strawberry, London Plane,

whatever will survive the streets,
the wind crouching at windowsills,
the small catastrophes of birds.

VI

He was trying to find noises for their words,
equivalents in bells, empty vessels, salted throats,
his daughters' laughter, re-building each signal

in from its edges like a bird's egg.
At Portaferry, round the coast,
there is broken crockery along the shore:

cargoes of tea sets dislodged from wrecks,
white leagues of tesserae, feet deep and scintillating
and giving out a low soughing underfoot,

palate music, soundings of table talk still to come.
Tiny shards fired, polished and entirely perfect,
the whole of the shore is broken crockery.

VII

Out in the air, geraniums,
flustered, breathing in for the first
the ripe carbon the traffic sheds
in a black microscopic snow

on a first-floor window ledge.
As if their muscles are feeding
on something incarnate in brick,
their small red bootees hammering.

VIII

It wouldn't have worked, a romance.
Apart from the tracks that I was
from the wrong side of or you were –

contemporaries but at odds
on most points; your dad's magistrate
comportment, his class, your custom

of doing well and doing good,
your good start, a face undarkened
yet by hurt or disappointment;

my intemperate livelihood,
bitter, angry, inconsistent,
mesmerised by the violent

as a fox stares down the headlights
bouncing gorgeously towards him
but making it sweet to the ditch,

my outrageous flirting with war,
your appointment with your cortège –
there was the fact we'd never met.

IX

When the albino boy,
some summer, in his shorts,
fell off the stable roof
into the big nettles
and brought the door with him,
banging down like a lid
to shut him in with them,
he squealed like a hedgehog,
wrestling with those swordsmen
till the big men freed him
by raising the drawbridge,
his white skin white with stings,
each inch of him nipped white
and swollen; but odder
still was that they coated

his whole self, toe to crown,
hair and all, with honey
that made the arrows
rise out and drop from him
like his own eyelashes,
as if they were called out
from him like Lazarus
to leave a mark on him
afterwards, and for good:
unclean because of fear
or suffering or wounds,
like one of those old saints,
exhumed, whose fingernails
broke on the coffin lid
but whose flesh still smelled sweet.

X

Your father lives alone in the fields.
He hasn't been to the city in years,
lives hand-to-mouth and takes his rest
along the range like a parlour tom,
measly shins all winter through.
As the seasons turn and it's warm again,
he's under the sky like a wanderer,
in the vineyard, on beds of leaves,
withered by years and simple grieving,
himself let go, hankering after you.

from The Odyssey, Bk XI

XI

A story tells that grain from Pharaoh's tomb
restored to the moist earth stirred itself,
reaching for the light of a laboratory lamp,
cracking its wrapping. And a lotus seed,

interred a millennium in a dry sea bed,
woke from its slumber as something monstrous,
misshapen, spotted by the centuries.
The bead of an Inca rattle a seed of canna lily.

Desperate somnolence. Waxy. Undead.
The man who spent so much time under sail
he had no house, let alone a garden,
hid cinders from the Cape between

the pages of his notebook like a lover
for botanists at Kew, a century after,
to rinse with soaking molecules of smoke –
the alchemy of bush fires making a desktop

a canopic jar of lights. The tiny tubers
broke into tongues: liparia villosa,
acacia, leucospermum, vivid, charmed,
heartbreaking as a lock of hair.

XII

It all went wrong that week. No matter how
one parses the sequence of what took place –
incompetence, without sanction or redress;
deliberate action settling slaughter;
or that mild attitude so drunk with arms
that all's forgiven in the face of it,
as usual (espoused by incident)
the dead deserving everything they get.

It is too far back to recall the sky's
demeanour or the quality of light
that April brought. But clearly the blouses
are out-of-style, shirt collars far too broad,

the cars knelt on the pavement already
preparing their red overcoats of rust,
the soldiers loping as they do in the past,
laden with gear that fits now in a palm.

XIII

And then the rain falls; and I know that if
it's raining in the town it's dry out there,
along the coast, by Strangford and Kilclief,

with the rocks burning black beyond repair.
The roads hold the tide by the aerodrome,
cups of salt water for the traveller

who has taken the longest route back home,
through air and earth and fire after take-off
in that order. The rain drops like a psalm.

XIV

For one moment in disturbance,
before discharge – your human face –
before the birds went up from trees
along those avenues like streams,

before the china cups returned
to saucers on the Lisburn Road,
new blouses, good shoes were betrayed
and physics worked, your human face

before your killer's should have seemed
as private and bold as guilty
meetings need: a shy distraction,
curious; familiar; safe.

XV

In time, one might remake everything,
a lifetime of the heart from unregarded things:
bird-song of broken china; ashes; bees.

The Hero

for Gail

I

For weeks (you recounted), he'd been consumed by water
and for no reason but to live in it, sour volume everywhere,

driven to travel under its roof: inflated alveoli,
cheeks ballooning like cherubs on medieval maps.

The surface above unravelled and ravelled,
as fulsome and as threadbare as thatch,

the light around below a procession of candles
and shadows of muscle and lungs strange prisoners

of the unnatural aquamarine at the pool bottom.
Cave light, laboratory life, a compelling discipline.

Above, the world stayed elusive, fugitive,
bottle-green; below, where his eyes were fixed,

the clarity stung. It was a kind of rehearsal
but still a mission; a task set; a pilgrimage to and fro

through the body of water full to its own brim
with silence and resistance and serious purpose.

The sides as he reached them were stations completed
by genuflection on smooth earth and a push back into suffering.

Was there nothing there below but his own self
dispersed in the silence, his blood everywhere?

There was the mania of his heart thundering in its element.
There was water and urine and disinfectant and chlorine

and many leagues to travel to where a miracle was waiting.

II

He found him on a paten of silver.
As he told it to you, the silty fog
was suddenly lifted and, settled far down,

a man on his knees was caught in a headlight
as if lowered down on a pallet of sunlight
to the only spot where he would be found.

A man was hung from his joints by the water's hands,
dandled by them, his own hands joined,
the whole of him swaying, grown organic and quiet.

As he told it to you, if that second eel
had not escaped by the skin of its teeth,
he wouldn't have raised his eyes to the lough

or heard 'My God, won't somebody help me'.
A sounding of mystery. Voices of the dead
singing along the coils of the waves,

broken and plaintive and almost missed.
It is a hard thing to swim in fresh water,
harder to kick out towards death itself,

against your will and your better judgement,
deliberately outwards then downwards alone,
away from the shore then inwards to loneliness.

III

A man walked into the lough to be drowned
and another walked after him because it was so.

One fell weeping and alone down the dull steps
of the real water into the cellar of the earth,

another went grimly down, sure-footed, stair by stair
after him, down to the conserving dark.

A saviour is marked on the outside
by the strength of his hands and on the inside

by the speed of his will and the ease with which
his ancestors people him so he can do no other

than step off the lifeboat, fall on the grenade,
climb out across No-Man's-Land with a last breath,

bristling, alarmed, devout, towards one man left alive.
Even the failures register with the universe, secretly.

So one fell weeping and alone and another went after him,
descending into hell through the harrowing currents

to the graceful strife of an absolute stranger,
embracing him, delivering him intact and perfect

and, after what seems like years, to astonished descendants
for whom one simple fact inflates like a lung into legend.

IV

There's not a year that he's not visited
by the parents of boys who pulled each other under
or the mother of a girl – strong swimmer, mind –
found pressed like a starfish to the rear window.

There's not a year that he's not consulted
on the nature and consequence of death by water
and all because he'd visited it; sojourned there;
came back. But did not come back alone.

Some Notes

Takabuti was the first Egyptian mummy to be brought to Ireland. She was brought to Belfast in 1834. Her hieroglyphs were deciphered by the Rev. Dr Edward Hincks of Killyleagh, Co. Down. On 27 August 2003, the body of Jean McConville was accidentally found by members of the public while they were walking on Shelling Hill beach in County Louth, Ireland. She had been killed by the IRA thirty one years previously.

~

The Orientalist Edward Hincks (1792-1866) was rector of Killyleagh from 1825 until his death on 3rd December 1866. Mr. Layard remarks: "It is to Dr. Hincks we owe the determination of the numerals, the name of Sennacherib on the monuments of Kouyunjik and of Nebuchadnezzar on the bricks of Babylon – three important and valuable discoveries."

~

Papers referenced here include 'On The Third Persepolitan Writing '(1848), 'On The Inscriptions at Van' (1850) and 'On The Khorsabad Inscriptions '(1850).

~

JMW Turner's 'The Flight into Egypt' depicts Mary, Joseph and the infant Christ fleeing into Egypt to escape King Herod. The broken Egyptian architecture half-submerged in the Nile recalls Turner's vaporous, romantic visions of Venice, and conveys a sense of faded power and crumbling prestige. In contrast to the ruined temples, a piercing ray of light appears to fall directly on the Christ child illuminating the new religion and the promise of salvation. The snake is a reference to Christ's triumph over the original sin of Adam and Eve in the Garden of Eden. Fortunately, the painting is one of the treasures of the Ulster Museum in Belfast.

~

When the British Museum in the 1840s received the massive wooden crates, which were shipped down the Persian Gulf into the Indian Ocean, down the east coast of Africa, past Madagascar, round the Cape of Good Hope and up the west coast of Africa into the Atlantic and on to London from Nineveh and Nimrud and Ur and Babylon, they were opened with crowbars to uncover clay tablets adorned with mysterious bird's-feet markings, those strange inscriptions.

The first thing they did was have rubbings taken of the tablets which were sent by train and mail coach and sailing ship to Newry first, and then by train and coach to a place as remote from London in those days as were the places those valuable cargoes had been loaded in the Near East. They shipped them to the door of a country parson in Lecale; a country parson who also happened to be one of the great scholars of the age.

~

'Gravity' -p77

Colum Marks (29) was shot dead by undercover police officers in a park at St Patrick's Avenue in Downpatrick, in April 1991. The site is now adjacent to a cinema complex.

Reading

Cathcart, K.J. (ed.): *The Edward Hincks Centenary Lectures* (Department of Near Eastern Languages, Dublin, 1994)

Cathcart, K.J. : *The Correspondence of Edward Hincks Vol. I (1818-1849)*, (University College Dublin Press, Dublin, 2007)

Cathcart, K.J. : *The Correspondence of Edward Hincks Vol II (1850-1856)*, (University College Dublin Press, Dublin 2008)

Daniels, Peter T. : 'Edward Hincks's decipherment of Mesopotamian cuneiform', in Cathcart, K.J. (ed.), *The Edward Hincks Centenary Lectures* (Department of Near Eastern Languages, Dublin, 1994)

Layard, Austen Henry: *The Ninevah Court in the Crystal Palace*, Elibron Classics (2005) Facsimile of the 1854 Crystal Palace Library edition.

Steegmuller, Frances : *Flaubert in Egypt: A Sensibility on Tour by Gustave Flaubert*, (Penguin Classics, 1996)

Younker, Randall W. :Institute of Archaeology, Andrews University, paper to Symposium: 'The Bible and Adventist Scholarship', Juan Dolio, Dominican Republic, March 19-26, 2000